VILLARD BOOKS TRADE PAPERBACKS
NEW YORK

Sh*t My Kids Ruined

An A–Z Celebration of Kid-Destruction

Julie Haas Brophy

To my sons, the inspiration for this work.
You're worth every challenge, any ruined things,
the lost sleep, and all the mess. I am enormously
proud you're my boys and I love you always.

A Villard Books Trade Paperback Original

Copyright © 2010 by Julie Haas Brophy

Published in the United States by Villard Books, an imprint of The Random
House Publishing Group, a division of Random House, Inc., New York.

VILLARD and "V" CIRCLED Design are registered trademarks of Random
House, Inc.

Library of Congress Cataloging-in-Publication Data
Brophy, Julie Haas.
    Sh*t my kids ruined : an A–Z celebration of kid-destruction / Julie Haas
Brophy.
        p.   cm.
    ISBN 978-0-345-52716-5 (pbk.)
    eBook ISBN 978-0-345-52718-9
    1. Parenting—Humor.   I. Title.
    PN6231.P2B76   2010
    818'.602—dc22   2010037948

Printed in the United States of America

www.villard.com

9 8 7 6 5 4 3 2 1

Book design by Susan Turner

WARNING

This book contains some sensitive, shocking, and funny personal images. A few are downright unpleasant. Gross, really! You are hereby advised not to view while eating, driving, operating heavy machinery, or enjoying sex. Though touted by some as a powerful visual birth control, its prophylactic effectiveness is not guaranteed.

INTRODUCTION

> **"When my kids become wild and unruly I use a nice safe playpen. When they're finished, I climb out."**
> —Erma Bombeck

Sh*t My Kids Ruined (SMKR) was born the morning of March 3, 2010. I was somewhat harried, doing too much at once, and my boys were going to be late for preschool. They were dressed and finishing their breakfasts, and in an attempt at efficiency, I set up materials for a project I planned to complete during the two hours they'd be at school. I make glass mosaic housewares in my few spare hours each week, and was preparing for upcoming local events.

I made two mistakes that morning: One, I placed my brushes, trays, frames, and covered paint can atop a newspaper and tarp on my rug. Not bright. Two, I turned my back for the seconds it took to place our dishes in the sink and grab my keys. I spun back around to a loud gasp that spilled from one of their mouths and that uh-oh facial expression saved only for spectacular disasters. My then two-year-old had snatched the paint can and emptied its contents in one fell swoop, and I was now looking at a quart of glossy black paint spreading over my rug.

Cue momentary breakdown. I don't know if the "nooooooooo" of disbelief was said aloud or in my head. For the next minute or two before getting ahold of myself, I was a whirlwind of misplaced yelling and irrational tears that can accompany exhaustion and frustration. There may even have been a few seconds of baboonlike jumping up and down. Maybe. I do remember the deep breaths and snapping a "You're not gonna believe this shit" picture with my phone, then dropping the boys off at school.

Though my son had technically carried out the spilling, the fault was clearly mine. After kicking myself repeatedly for having left the paint out to begin with, I uploaded the photo to Facebook. I was already in the habit of photographing and posting things that amused me, occasionally including the minutiae of my life. In the trapped isolation and discomfort I often felt as a new mom and reluctant suburbanite, Facebook served at times as an ideal outlet. I tended to post when procrastinating or feeling silly or bored, or in this case, seeking both comfort and laughs.

Comments regarding the rug photo poured in—parents commiserated and chuckled, child-free friends guffawed and teased. With each new remark I smiled. I laughed! I wasn't alone with my paint-blob misery; I was virtually supported (and ribbed mercilessly) by friends near and far. Even though the rug incident left me upset, these comments helped me turn around a crappy morning. And though I loved the rug—I'd bought it years earlier on eBay for not much money—it was already quite threadbare. My struggle was with my frustration and my sense of powerlessness, not with the loss of anything valuable.

The same morning, I ran into a friend on my block who'd seen the picture. And in the sophisticated manner for which I'm known, I complained laughingly to her, "They ruin all of my shit!"

With that phrase rattling around in my head, I returned home and searched for domain names. In minutes I'd purchased ShitMyKidsRuined.com, and after a key suggestion from my brother Brian, added the Pets equivalent later that morning. Not long afterward, Husband and Wife joined the family of Ruined websites. After all, when I said "they" ruin my stuff, I was including all four beloved crap-trashing males with whom I'm living (husband, boys, pug).

Later that day, I used my phone to photograph everything I could recall one or both boys staining, breaking, ripping, or somehow affecting adversely. As you may imagine I didn't have trouble finding many items in this category. For starters there was our off-white upstairs couch, our home's only other victim of truly stunning destruction, this one at the hands of our older son, then three. The night before we were going on a trip, he'd snuck out of bed and into my handbag where he found a permanent marker, red nail polish, and zit cream. And with this thoroughly damaging trio he graffitied one side of the couch, which, incidentally, was made of canvas. Blank canvas.

The next obvious candidates for my gallery of crapped-up possessions (most of which are still in use) included a decimated laptop, yogurt-stained lamp shade, warped cabinet door, broken toilet paper holder, backless remote control, torn window blinds, and just about every pop-up book that had the misfortune to pass through our home. I posted these images together in an album online.

The next day my friend Sara, who loved the idea from the get-go, walked me through the basics of weblogging. She got me started on Tumblr (where SMKR spent its first four months), and she helped me understand things like Twitter and site analytics, which hitherto caused my eyes to glaze over. Sara also provided my first site photo that was not my own—a fabulous photo of her dog whose white fur had red marker streaks courtesy of her youngest son.

Within the day, more friends as well as strangers began submitting pictures of their family's kid-destruction. Anonymously revealing these private, often unpleasant, sometimes embarrassing moments proved therapeutic and fun, and word spread. Remarkable images representing depleted sleep, stretch-marked bellies, and devastated bank accounts joined the pictures of Sharpie-marked walls, abused electronics, mangled broken toys. No blame, no bitterness. Just comic relief.

More positive response and enthusiasm led to a group of friends on Facebook each placing the SMKR link to their personal pages. I set up a fan page that quickly collected members who posted photos and comments with great frequency and fervor. Site hits doubled. Then tripled. Communities on Facebook, Twitter, and Tumblr grew exponentially by the day.

All of a sudden, and best of all, moms and dads were writing to me daily saying how much they appreciated, loved, or related to the site. Parents wrote on the Facebook fan page, "I've found my people!!" I received all sorts of photo submissions, which were clever and hilarious, relatable and occasionally shocking. Fans created representations of destroyed libidos, kid-interrupted phone calls, a spoiled love for cooking. SMKR developed into a place where it was okay to bemoan and joke and laugh together about the child-bearing-related body changes as well, which too often feel taboo to discuss openly.

Then things got completely crazy. I was receiving requests for radio interviews from New York to Dublin to Sydney. Bloggers started writing for permission to post SMKR photos on their own sites and link to mine. *Entertainment Weekly*'s Pop Watch Blog wrote about it, followed by Jane Wells on her CNBC.com blog. In addition to being featured on numerous humor and parenting sites, SMKR was covered on a zany and disparate array of media outlets from The Huffington Post to *Sports Illustrated* online to Gizmodo to maltastar.com to roughfisher.com.

The *New York Times* writer Susan Dominus wrote about the site in her column, Big City, and the intensity of interest in SMKR magnified again. That week saw nearly two million page views. Agents, editors, publishers, television producers, tech people, advertisers, web designers, and even a clothing manufacturer reached out to me. It was surreal. The next month the *Wall Street Journal* online ran a piece about the site. ABC's *Good Morning America* did an anchor chat segment. And in late June, Time.com named Shit My Kids Ruined one of the best blogs of 2010, also featuring it in a video about five blogs *Time* writers read daily. Wait. What?!

I lived half-convinced the crew from *Candid Camera* or *Punk'd* would jump out at any moment. How had this simple, moderately crass photo blog gotten to this position? I was in utter disbelief, despite how very real and serious some of it started to become. In late May, I signed with a literary agent. By mid-June, I'd submitted a book proposal. And in early July, I got the thrilling news I'd be writing this book!! Just one thing: It had to be completed by mid-August. Wait. What?!

Because meanwhile, back on Earth, the transition was awkward. My life was in disarray and my house a pigsty (though I suppose pugsty is more accurate). I'd started the site as a lark and never took seriously the possibility that it would have this sort of trajectory. My sudden inheritance of a behemoth new job, which would leave me without any family prep-time, was difficult on everyone. You can't imagine the laundry and dishes, the unanswered emails and calls, and the piles of crap of all sorts that accumulated. Actually, many of you can, because you're busy parents, too.

It's the same with SMKR. While some of the site's fans love it purely for the laughs, many of you have shared that it's also the camaraderie that keeps so many of you coming back. Well, that and the unusual view into the private sphere of other families' lives and homes—the peek at the unedited, the messy, the ugly.

SMKR photos don't often depict our best moments. They're not usually our proudest snapshots. Our children are sometimes presented in an unflattering way. In other shots our parenting doesn't always come across as all that stellar, either. In these pictures we are vulnerable, exposed. We are real. And SMKR makes no assumptions about the lives of those whose pictures are contained within. I know very well from my own experience that snapshots of one's worst family moments do not represent that family's normal existence.

When we're guests in someone else's house, we usually

experience that space in a somewhat inauthentic, spiffed-up-for-company state. In private, however, that same home may be scattered with kid debris, piled shoes, mail, jackets, books, towels, dishes, laundry, newspapers, et cetera. When I am expecting guests, for example, I turn the stained or ripped sides of lampshades toward the wall. (Incidentally, I used to *replace* lampshades, which I finally realized is kinda futile.)

The same phenomenon is true concerning many families' photos. Usually, the ones to which we're privy are the shiny ones—Christmas card pictures, framed mantel portraits, class photos, and albums of carefully selected images—showing everyone in their most flattering light.

Well not in these photos, baby!

SMKR, like child-rearing itself, oscillates from the funny to the disgusting to the heartwarming to the maddening, with stops at embarrassing, scary, and joyous. It shines a spotlight on some of the unsightly, gooey, and tougher aspects of parenting, and celebrates them. And if possible, learns from them. Think of it as a lost chapter of *What to Expect When You're Expecting*. It embodies the out-of-control nature of parenting. SMKR comprises all the things either no one ever told you or you couldn't possibly have understood until you lived it. Every. Single. Day.

Ed Asner once said, "Raising kids is part joy and part guerrilla warfare." Amen, Mr. Asner! The seldom-uttered truth is that parenting, while easily the most extraordinary and worthwhile experience of my life, can be a drag or a battle, and a lonely one at that. *Shit My Kids Ruined* is my effort to come to grips with and laugh through parenting adversity.

In terms of what kids have ruined, most obviously, there's the physical—the mauled belongings, awful messes, painful injuries, destroyed electronics, poopsplosions, crashed cars. There's also an emotional component of the personal changes—growing into a new level of responsible adulthood, deferring one's own needs for another's, and becoming accustomed to being depended upon, and accepting our altered bodies affected by the ravages of reproduction.

On and off throughout parenthood thus far, I've battled two main difficulties, which happen to occur simultaneously. One is the sometimes painful, totally awkward mourning of my pre-baby self—my body, my freedom, my world as I'd known it for thirty plus years. The second is the totally awkward, sometimes painful metamorphosis into my new role and identity as mom of two and suburbanite.

Parents have flocked to SMKR seeking comic relief, and like me, have found salvation through empathy and laughter. Swapping stories and uploading pictures is social, therapeutic, and fun, and it's made SMKR both wonderfully sophomoric and a meaningful community. Sharing anecdotes is strongly encouraged, whether they're submitted with or without a photo. One mom wrote, "We call our son Captain Destructo. He used to be Sergeant Destructo, but we've promoted him." And like us and the li'l Sergeant's parents, your culprits have names you've shared: "Not Me," "I Didn't," "No One," "I Don't Know." In our home, the sneakiest recurring perpetrator is named "No, He Did It."

To my delight, grandparents have become active members of the SMKR community, too. And let me tell you, while this group completely adores their grandkids, you've never read more gleeful sentiments about the ability to pass 'em right back to mom and dad at the end of a visit! One grandma wrote of her daughter's destructiveness as a girl and admitted a tinge of enjoyment in watching her daughter struggle with toddlers of her own. She added, "Karma's a bitch!"

I've come to find out this material *really* amuses and horrifies the child-free set. This group's enjoyment of SMKR has been an enormous surprise to me and I love it. It's all a trade-off, right? I'm thrilled and grateful I have kids despite some of the downers captured in this book. And I know those without kids lead joyous, meaningful lives *and* enjoy your intact things! I'm a firm believer that kids are not for everyone, and to the extent that SMKR has affirmed your decision not to "breed" (as some in the child-free community call it), I'm genuinely pleased. And schadenfreude certainly has its place. I say laugh it up, people!

SMKR is appreciated by many of you for its tone, which has a little bite, but is mostly goofy, supportive, bemused. Steve James Snyder wrote in his piece about SMKR on Time.com that the site "feels less like a compilation of scowls than smirks," with which I agree. And this is very much by design. SMKR is a comic tribute to the madness of child rearing as well as a venting mechanism. I am only interested in the project if there's an affectionate and nonjudgmental voice at its core.

SMKR is not for criticism or told-you-so's. As in the case of my ruined rug incident, it's pretty clear from many of your photos that the parent or caregiver may well have screwed up, too. A man once commented on the site, "I'm going to start a sister site and name it 'I Wasn't Watching My Kids.com,' " which at first mortified me and I debated deleting it. But when I put my defensiveness aside, I was able to see it as very funny and decided it had a place in the discourse of SMKR. I wound up printing the comment (as I've done for all of my favorites), and it's been on my wall for months, causing me to roll my eyes or smile depending on my mood.

Most parents I know would agree that 100 percent supervision of their children is next to impossible to achieve. In the course of a day with small children, one has to take the occasional gamble. Perhaps you have bathroom needs, a laundry cycle to shift, a phone call or doorbell to answer. At those instances, if the children are playing nicely or otherwise occupied, it's reasonable to seize the moment and dash. And mostly this works out great! Mostly.

The majority of you seem to live in the same world as I do. That is, it's my experience that even the most engaged, fabulous, and attentive parents will miss preventing the occasional disaster. Wonderful, responsible parents make mistakes. And even the most obedient, perfectly nurtured child blows it now and again. Thirty seconds of unsupervised time is all it can take! It's quite impressive, really.

This is not about fault or blame. A huge number of SMKR images depict chaos and destruction, but none exhibit genuine malice. In fact, as often as our kids are the culprits, sometimes parents themselves do quite a bit of the ruining. "You know the people who are always sure about the proper way to raise children? Those who've never had any." Tell 'em, Bill Cosby! I was the greatest parent in the world until I had kids. I've come to find out I'm exceedingly human and my idea of what constitutes great parenting has evolved.

As you know, the name of my site and this book came about as a result of actual ruined items, but the definition quickly evolved to include many creative usages. Technically, of course, many of the items herein are not actually ruined. As I've mentioned, most of the items in my "ruined" things album are still in use in our home. The word is a shorthand way of saying "messed up" somehow, and one cannot take most of the entries in this book literally—its title could just as easily have been called *Bummers in Parenthood*.

It did come awfully close to being called *"Stuff" My Kids Ruined*. I was not comfortable using *shit* in the name, but I assured myself that few people beyond my circle of friends would ever even see my site. Whoops! I still blush frequently when asked the name of my site or book.

I feel the need to remind you: This is NOT a serious book. I grant you it brushes against some serious topics. But it's listed under Humor and Family. I say this primarily to the few of you who have written to me in outrage over one of any number of issues that, frankly, you've taken far too seriously. SMKR's stated mission is "Commiseration, Comic Relief, and Birth Control." And that is all. This crap's fer laughin'!

And as Steve James Snyder asked rhetorically on Time.com, "What is a parent to do but shrug, laugh it off, and share pics with fellow parents who can nod along in bemused sympathy?" Don't know about you, but I'm not sure I could endure raising small children without laughing frequently and heartily about the whole crazy, poignant, hilarious, and profound experience.

". . . our **ability to sleep in.** This was all done by 7:30 AM." *Submitted by: Ruth*

"I think our kids probably figured our **alarm clock** was obsolete since they always wake us before it goes off anyhow." *Submitted by: Michelle*

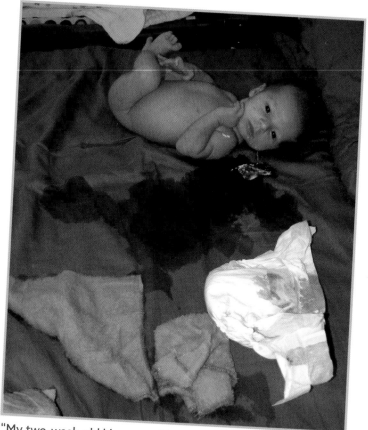

"My two-week-old blew out of his diaper while I was nursing him, covering me and him in orange sticky poop. I was cleaning us both with wipes when he peed all over his face and the bed. I picked him up, thinking he was surely done, but no, he proceeded to pee again all over my lap. I laid him back down to go start the bath water (wipes just weren't gonna cut it) and he barfed all over the bed." *Submitted by: Alicia*

"Two words: Alone time." *Submitted by: Tim*

"Lindzey's arm and the beginning of the summer! Two breaks, two bones, one arm."
Submitted by: Megan

Atmosphere   *Submitted by: Bevin*

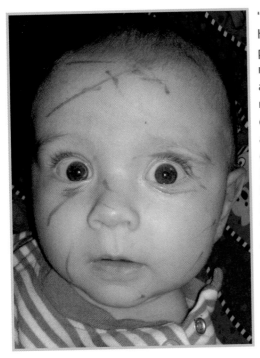

"I saw my two-and-a-half-year-old take felt pens into the living room. I followed him after one minute to make sure he was drawing in the notebook and not on the table. I didn't see any drawings in the notebook, or on the table. And then I saw his baby brother's face."
Submitted by: Kat

"My back!" *Submitted by: Bill*

Basketball backboard "No, son. You're supposed to throw the *ball*." *Submitted by: Brian*

Bangs *Submitted by: Heather*

BBQ plans "The picture speaks for itself. I never even got to use the chairs or the umbrella, all still wrapped in the original plastic!"
Submitted by: Tasha

Beanbag chair
Submitted by:
Rebecca

Bedspread
"This is what happens when grandma gives you a Sharpie."
Submitted by: Dianne

"My son loved to sneak out of the house when he was a toddler. I installed sled **bells** on every window and door, so I would hear his escape attempts before they became successful. This worked quite well all the way through his teen years."
Tip submitted by: Victoria

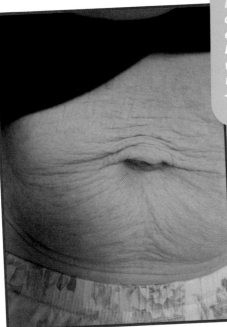

Belly
"Three years ago I was twenty-eight and had a flat, smooth stomach . . . the boys ruined any chances of me ever pursuing a career as a bikini model." *Submitted by: Leigh*

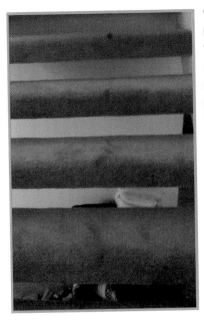

"We were moving in . . . we hadn't been there an hour. Two-year-old totally entertained by sliding down steps on her butt . . . we had no idea there was a surprise inside. Did I mention it was brand new carpet?! And I only had about six baby wipes to clean her and the mess." *Submitted by: Erica*

"I'm assuming it would be in bad taste to put a picture of my saggy boobs on here, huh?" *Submitted by: Sellah*

Brick wall "Age fifteen. Driving school dropout." *Submitted by: Amy*

"My brand new bronzer . . . this was the day after my son squirted toothpaste all over the bathroom."
Submitted by: Brittany

Bunk bed "This is just another day in the life of two boys under the age of seven. Good times."
Submitted by: Jennifer

"Our pull-out cabinet."
Submitted by: Beth

"I would take pictures of what my kids ruined, but it was the camera."
Submitted by: Chris

"Never lend your **car** to anyone to whom you have given birth."
—Erma Bombeck

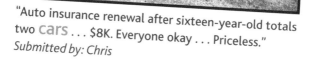

"Auto insurance renewal after sixteen-year-old totals two **cars** . . . $8K. Everyone okay . . . Priceless."
Submitted by: Chris

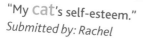

"My cat's self-esteem."
Submitted by: Rachel

"**Cleaning** your house while the kids are still growing is like shoveling the walk before it stops snowing."
—Phyllis Diller

"My son, who has a scientist for a father, decided to do a science experiment. What happens when you put a cell phone in the microwave for two minutes? You have to buy a new cell phone. And microwave." *Submitted by: Hannah*

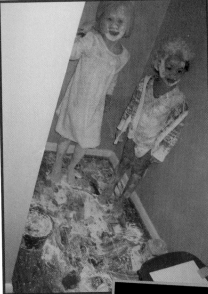

Central air system

"What these pictures don't show is that they are right next to the AC intake vent. It was seventeen months ago and I'm still finding cornstarch in random places!"
Submitted by: Hamburke

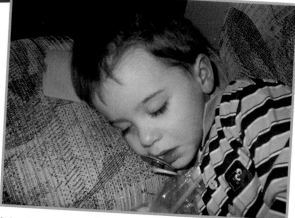

"That's a slice of cheese under his head."
Submitted by: Lori

"I have a great way to child-proof your house. If you are a woman, get your tubes tied. Problem solved!"
Submitted by: Sandy N.

"I learned this child-proofing tip when my sister had her first Christmas as a walking toddler . . . my dad hooked the **Christmas tree** to the ceiling so she wouldn't mess with it. Wish I had photographic evidence today, it left a lasting impression."

Tip submitted by: Stephanie

"Here's my son in the **closet** we gave him so he might not draw on ALL the walls! It's at least cut it down. It seems odd to tell him 'crayons and markers in the closet!' "

Tip submitted by: Melissa F.

"Oh no, not the coffee." *Submitted by: Alyssa*

"Destroyed my **computer screen**, closed it back up, and I didn't find it until the next day."
Submitted by: Jojo

"The quickest way for a parent to get a child's attention is to sit down and look **comfortable**."
—Lane Olinhouse

"My **confidence**."
Submitted by: Ally

"Yes, that is his sister covered in glitter in the background. And, 'A couch?' you ask. Yes, that is my couch also covered in glitter, 'the herpes of crafting supplies.' "
Submitted by: Charlotte

Countertop "FYI, if you mix all the food dyes together you get this lovely green shade."
Submitted by: Edward

Dad's self-esteem
"Yes, that's a drawing of daddy. And yes, daddy has man-boobs."
Submitted by: Heather

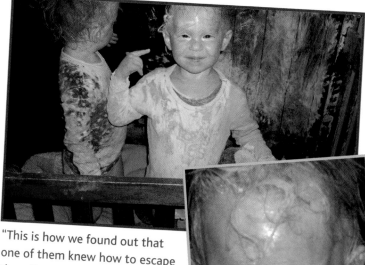

"This is how we found out that one of them knew how to escape the crib. She crawled out and got a tub—not a tube—of **Desitin**."
Submitted by: Steve

Dessert "Apparently the first bite is the best."
Submitted by: Kari

Dignity "Words are not necessary to explain this picture."
Submitted by: Christie

" 'Mom can't see us. We are ninjas,' was the phrase that tempted me to check out what was going on in the **dining room**."
Submitted by: Nicole

Dinner Time
Submitted by: Skye

Diploma "When your child gets really quiet while playing in your bedroom closet, be afraid. Mine dug this out of a box in my closet and got creative while her grandmother was watching her. Thanks, Maw Maw."
Submitted by: Jenilee

Display "When you finally decide to go shopping for yourself, this is what your two-year-old does."
Submitted by: Stephanie

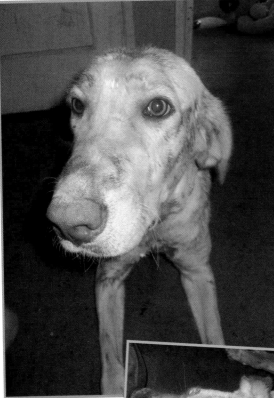

"My five-year-old son made our **dog** pretty."
Submitted by: The Weiss Family

"Raise your hand if you've ever had to hose down a complete **doll house** painted with poo!" [hand raised]
Submitted by: Melanie

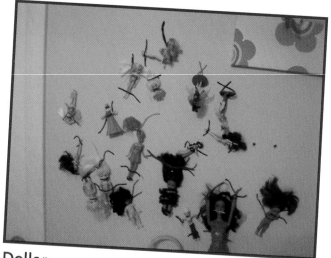

Dolls "Barbies + those wicky-stick things = The Wall of Evil. They spent hours perfecting the Wall of Evil. I'm saving up for their future therapy bills."
Submitted by: JAS

"My son swung his backpack into the $400 'unbreakable' **door** . . . and broke it."
Submitted by: Suzie

"The top **drawer** of my bathroom vanity filled to the brim with hot water after my three-year-old needed to wash his hands (coincidentally after drawing all over the table with markers). Two weeks later I wondered why the heating duct in the floor wasn't working. It was full of water." *Submitted by: Renee*

"Carved into the top of a $1,200 **dresser**!"
Submitted by: Trish

"Duct Tape."
Tip submitted by: Abigail

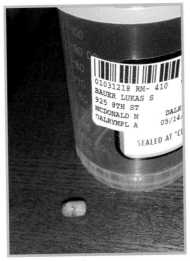

"My son had to have full-blown surgery to have this rock removed from his ear."
Submitted by: Trina

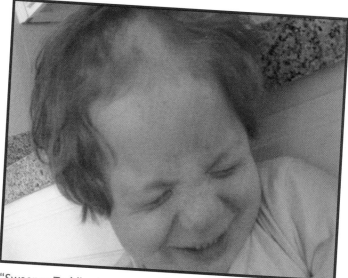

"Sweeney Toddler here ruined Easter family portraits."
Submitted by: Missi

"I think I'll just say delivering my babies affected my, um, elasticity. Goooo Kegels!"
Submitted by: Jen

"First the dog buried the plastic eggs in the backyard. Then my four-year-old decided to wash them in the bathroom sink. And then somehow they fell into the toilet, and someone closed the lid and walked away."
Submitted by: Candace

Entryway "With a gallon of milk."
Submitted by: James

Evening "I first saw the body paint when she came around the corner—after which she explained that she chose purple, black, and yellow for the television." *Submitted by: Allison*

Exercise "My two-year-old grandson decided to play with the mustard. His four-year-old brother ran off to get his mom with mustard all over his feet and also ruined the carpet." *Submitted by: Candice*

Expectations *Submitted by: Cassandra*

"My eye! She poked it. Hard." *Submitted by: Jenny S.*

"Her eyebrows." *Submitted by: Jennifer*

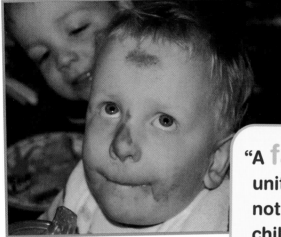

Face "Callan, pushed over by brother Fletcher."
Submitted by: Richard

"A **family** is a unit composed not only of children but of men, women, an occasional animal, and the common cold."
—Ogden Nash

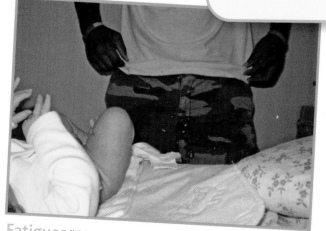

Fatigues "I'd never seen an explosive BM until this. You would have thought her dad would have learned to stay out of the line of fire." *Submitted by: O.M.*

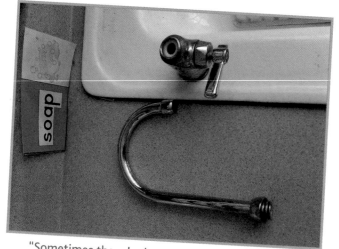

"Sometimes they don't even have to be your own kids to wreak havoc in your life. Here's a picture of the sink my students 'fixed' for me. They broke the bolt, too, so the entire faucet had to be replaced."
Submitted by: Rebecca

"Managed to render supersized bag of cat food and fertilizer useless simultaneously." *Submitted by: James*

Ficus tree "My three-and-a-half-year-old and her best friend were pretending to be 'hungry giraffes'—the tree was almost dead three months ago, and it was just starting to make a comeback." *Submitted by: Catherine*

"I'd post a picture of my dead fish, but that's just creepy." *Submitted by: Steven*

"My one-and-a-half-year-old threw an empty plastic toy bin at the forty-inch flatscreen tv my husband has waited a long time for and purchased just six days ago. Sorry, honey!!!" *Submitted by: Marie*

Floor "Oh your guests are arriving any minute? Well I got the party started by dancing in my own poo!"
Submitted by: Nicole

"Fun physics lesson for five-year-olds at our house a month ago: What happens when one forty-five-pound boy climbs out his sister's window and onto the flowerbox?"
Submitted by: Erin

"My Friday night—Parents of school-age kids will know exactly what is going on in this picture." *Submitted by: Katherine*

"Frame the wall drawings."
Tip submitted by: Merrill

"My garage door was ruined when my sons discovered they could hatchet-throw forks at it. (Also ruined: a set of silverware.)" *Submitted by: Erin*

"It took us a whole morning to tidy the garden, sweep the patio, and sow four pots full of lovely flower seeds. She managed to destroy it all in the time it took to wash my hands."
Submitted by: Morgan

Glass "I checked the receipt. This happened sixty-eight minutes after I got through the checkout lane with the ball and the bat." *Submitted by: Julie*

"A truly appreciative child will break, lose, spoil, or fondle to death any really successful gift within a matter of a few minutes."
—Russell Lynes

"Peanut butter, mayonnaise, and vegetable oil are great for getting gum out of hair, even Mommy's!"
Tip submitted by: Crystal

"My hair. He put the Thomas train on my head and turned it on. Ouch!" *Submitted by: Jane*

Hallway
Submitted by: Loretta

On **health**:
"Last week I got a flu that I caught, 'cause my daughter coughed into my mouth."
—Louis CK

"Me: Cameron why did you color your hand blue?
Cameron: I was drawing a spider.
Me: Why did you color your whole hand?
Cameron: I was squishing the spider!"
Submitted by: Jessica

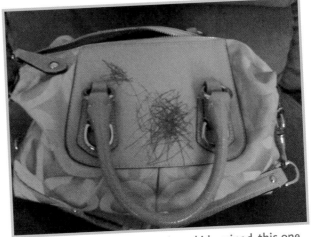

"Of all the things one of my three kids ruined, this one
breaks my heart the most. Good-bye $300 handbag!"
Submitted by: Amber

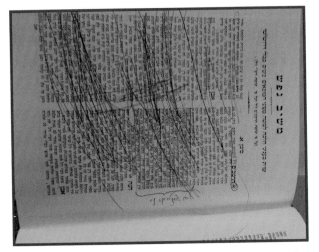

Hebrew text "What you're looking at is a rare volume of rabbinic law that my three-year old daughter edited."
Submitted by: Steven

"She mutilated my holiday cupcakes and now I have nothing to bring to the party. Thanks, sweetie."
Submitted by: Serena

Hood "Pee Shit Poop" *Submitted by: Anonymous*

12/10/2005

"My two older boys (I have three, what were we thinking?) were washing the van and decided to put the hose in the ground . . . they couldn't get it out. After much mud, dad had to cut the hose."
Submitted by: Penny

Hound "My twelve-year-old was helping me make his lunch for school. If he wanted hot dogs, he should have said so."
Submitted by: Shani

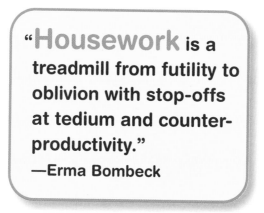

"**Housework** is a treadmill from futility to oblivion with stop-offs at tedium and counter-productivity."
—Erma Bombeck

Ice pops "Just glad I saw these before they all melted. Too bad I didn't see the ones melted on the top bunk."
Submitted by: Carol

Icing sugar "This was my birthday surprise—my then fourteen-year-old, her best friend, and my eight-year-old son decided to make cupcakes to celebrate. How sweet—you'd think. This is the kitchen they left me."
Submitted by: Kaz

"Only buy IKEA."
Tip submitted by: Johnna

Inkpad "Blue stamp pad . . . he ate it." *Submitted by: Filva*

"**Insomnia**: A contagious disease often transmitted from babies to parents."
—Shannon Fife

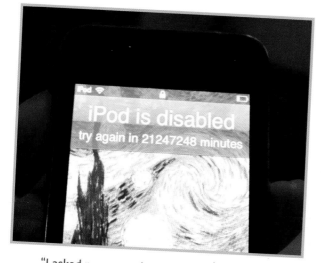

"I asked my son to bring me the iPod . . . in the time it took him to walk across the room, he disabled my iPod for thirty-nine YEARS. I'll be seventy-nine before it unlocks."
Submitted by: Carly

"iPod touch + open bathroom door = a hard lesson learned."
Submitted by: Tiffany

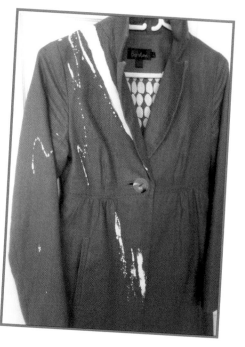

J key "Sorry *enny, *ason, and *ustin. The five-year-old ate your initial." *Submitted by: Isabelle*

Jacket "My two-year-old decided my brand-new-have-only-worn-it-once coat would look better covered in Liquid Paper/White-Out." *Submitted by: Rachel*

"Li'l Jackson
Pollock's
jeans."
Submitted by:
Mark

"As a housewife, I feel
that if the kids are still
alive when my husband
gets home from work,
then hey, I've done my
job."
—Roseanne Barr

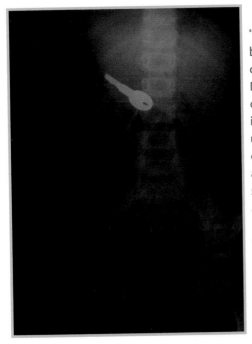

"When my son was a baby, I got sick of him dumping out all of the DVDs from my media cabinet so I put a lock on it. That worked out great until he turned five years old, climbed on top of it, and inexplicably swallowed the key. They assured us it would, uh, pass. Two weeks, three trips to the emergency room, and $2,500 later, they had to put him under and fish it out through his throat."
Submitted by: Katy

"We found him secretly plucking out keys from the computer keyboard using a butter knife."
Submitted by: Chris

Kitchen ceiling
"Okay, kids, let's make some tomato sauce!"
Submitted by: Raphaël

Kitchen floor
"Courtesy of my mischievous three-year-old twin boys."
Submitted by: Twila

Lampshade
Submitted by:
J.P.B.

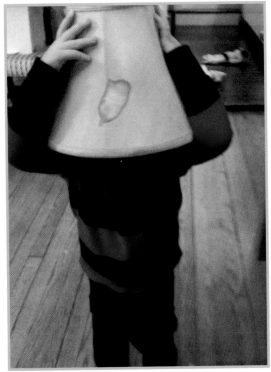

"Butter laptop. Oh, how we laughed." *Submitted by: Jansen*

Laundry. "Not really *ruined*, but a pain in the ass to clean up." *Submitted by: Jennifer*

"After flooding the lawn to the point of mud pit, they turned the hose on their uncle, who was lying on a nearby hammock talking on the phone." *Submitted by: Paul*

Leather "Apparently, our four-year-old twin girls have been 'drawing' on it with their fingernails. Awesome."
Submitted by: Jennifer

Leftovers "My kid reheated some french fries in the microwave. She left the fries in the Styrofoam container from the restaurant. She cooked them for seven minutes and seventy-seven seconds because seven is her favorite number."
Submitted by: Brad

"The most remarkable thing about my mother is that for thirty years she served the family nothing but leftovers. The original meal has never been found."
—Calvin Trillin

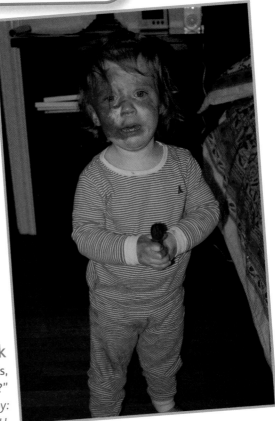

Lipstick
"My real question is, why is *she* crying?"
Submitted by:
Jennifer H.

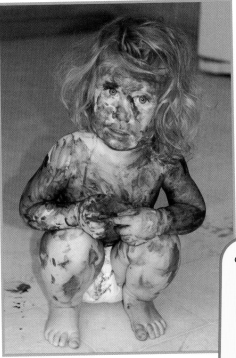

Little sister
"This is NOT poop—it's paint! I have to say that first. This is simply the way my oldest expressed herself this particular day, using her little sister as her blank canvas."
Submitted by: Chrissie

"**The first half of our lives are ruined by our parents and the second half by our children.**"
—**Clarence Day**

"When we stayed at hotels with our small children, I was always trying to stay one step ahead of them. The bathrooms there have no windows, but they do have door **locks!** I made it a practice to keep a towel folded over the top of the door. The toddler couldn't pull it down and the door could not be closed tightly. This prevents the child locked in the bathroom and screaming hysterically scenario."
Tip submitted by: Cheryl

MacBook "At least four magnets shoved in. No longer operational." *Submitted by: Wes*

"Her daddy's manhood." *Submitted by: Nicole*

Meal "Uh, I think this one is pretty self-explanatory."
Submitted by: Devon

Messes? "When your toddler makes a mess strewn room-wide—I'm talking the wall-to-wall type—your back likely cannot handle all the bending. GET A BROOM. Sweep all that stuff into one big pile and put a trash bag, toy bucket, and laundry hamper next to yourself. Then pop a squat and start digging."

Tip submitted by: Breanna

Photo submitted by: Courtney

Microwave "My son states he was running through the kitchen when this gem happened. I kinda believe him, though, since he scalped himself a little when he did it."
Submitted by: Emily

"People often ask me, 'What's the difference between couplehood and babyhood?' In a word? Moisture. Everything in your life is now more moist. Between your spittle, your diapers, your spit-up and drool, you get your baby food, your wipes, your formula, your leaky bottles, sweaty baby backs, and numerous untraceable sources—all creating an ever-present moistness in my life, which heretofore was mainly dry."
—Paul Reiser

I love you, Mom.
I can not say
how much I
love you. I can
not love you
more. But... you
are ugly. ♡♡♡
♡♡♡
♡♡♡

Mom's self-esteem "My six-year-old ruined my chance of convincing my wife I had nothing to do with this Mother's Day card this year." *Submitted by: Rob*

"Why yes, that is my **mop** filled with two liters of milk." *Submitted by: Danica*

"While I realize of course if was for him, he ruined *my* mural when he added another spaceship!" *Submitted by: J.P.B.*

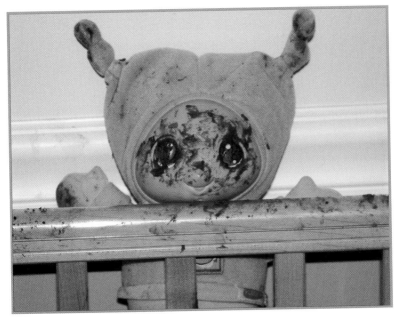

Naptime "This is what my twenty-month-old did to her Glow Worm!! Yes, that is what you think it is." *Submitted by: Julie*

"My children killed my **nerves** from the moment they became mobile. Oh, who am I kidding? My nerves were shot when they were in utero." *Submitted by: Michelle*

"The boy who ate **New Zealand**: My son chews on paper. Notice he carefully tore off all along the bottom before giving in to temptation and eating the islands." *Submitted by: Sara*

"My daughter broke my husband's **nose** by accidently head-butting him right before Christmas. While he was bleeding profusely, she was worried about a small scratch on her forehead!" *Submitted by: Laura*

Nuptials "In about 20 years or so I intend to get even!"
Submitted by: Melanie

Office "At least they are cute." *Submitted by: Sara*

Office walls "All of a sudden the house got really quiet. TOO quiet. And my spouse asked, 'Where's Andrew?!' "
Submitted by: Gretchen

"We scored a major food bonanza when somebody gave us a gallon jar of olives. They lasted twenty minutes before ending up everywhere. One month later and the kitchen still smells like a Greek restaurant."
Submitted by: Edward

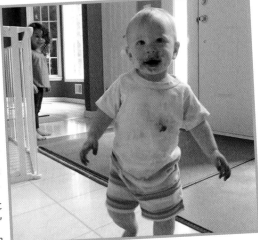

"Never let your three-year-old watch your one-year-old while you get dressed."
Submitted by: Dan

Organization
Submitted by: Paul

"I've noticed that one thing about parents is that no matter what stage your child is in, the parents who have **older children** always tell you the next stage is worse."
—Dave Barry

Outgoing package
Submitted by: Ashley

Outing
"Does Culvers need a spokeskid?"
Submitted by: Teri

Oven "I love my kids but . . . ! !"
Submitted by: Julie S.

"*Dawn detergent is really great at removing* **paint** *from carpet, fans, walls, hair, and the body.*"

Tip submitted by: Crystal
Photo submitted by: Mary

"**Parents** **are the bones on which children cut their teeth.**"
—Peter Ustinov

"This used to be my five-foot- tall **peach tree** until one afternoon when my four-year-old and his friend decided it was a 'monster tree.' "
Submitted by: Brittany

"My daughter has eaten every **pencil** in the house."
Submitted by: Judith

"My three-year-old thought our fish would enjoy an entire container of **pepper**!"
Submitted by: Sarah

Perishables
"Everyone knows that cottage cheese, hummus, eggs, and butter are the cornerstones of any great structure."
Submitted by: Todd

"Family **photo day** at Sears. The beast wanted to be in every picture!" *Submitted by: John*

Piano "The first time I looked at photos on your site, I thought to myself, 'These parents must have left their kids unsupervised for hours for them to do something like that. Well, we left our two-year-old son to play in the next room for, what, like, five minutes? Behold the destruction." *Submitted by: Nicola*

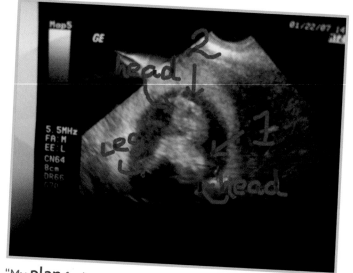

"My **plan** for 'one more baby'." *Submitted by: Bonnie*

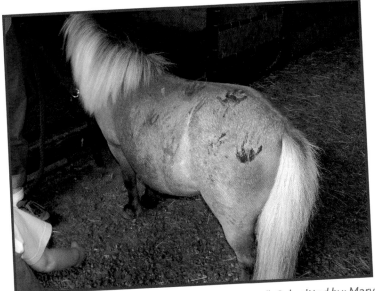

"The poor **pony** . . . he will never be the same." *Submitted by: Marvel*

"Yes, a **potted plant** was way too close (apparently) to the eating area, grrr."
Submitted by: Sally

On possessions:
"If you love it, DON'T buy it."
Tip submitted by: Rebecca

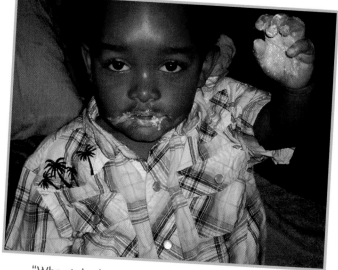

"Who stole the package of **powdered donuts**?"
Submitted by: Jane

"I waited until the night before the first Christmas gathering to wrap and put **presents** under the tree because I knew my three-year-old would have a hard time resisting. I stayed up late to get all of them wrapped. When my son woke up the next morning he was so excited to see them all, and we had several discussions about how they weren't all for him and he needed to wait. Not an hour after I left for work I got this picture on my phone—every single one unwrapped!"

Submitted by: Molly

Princess
"Someday my prince will come with a towel and some glue."

Submitted by: Julia

"Our beautiful **professional pictures** . . . then again, we thought it was so funny, we ended up buying multiple copies of this one!!"
Submitted by: Ryan
Image courtesy of Natasha Duckwall

Punctuality "My plans to be *on time!*" Be advised . . . our kids can *still* get into things when seat-belted in the car seat!!"
Submitted by: Susan

"So the **puppy** walks into my office and has a wet head. I innocently inquire, 'Why is Hadie wet?' To which my five-year-old says about his three-year-old brother, 'Hyland peed on her head.' Duh! Of course! I should have known." *Submitted by: Kelley*

"The queen of freakin' England. She had a solar panel on her handbag that fueled her famous wave. A state funeral is in order, methinks." *Submitted by: Barbara*

Quiche-making plans
Submitted by: Amanda

"**The truth is that parents are not really interested in justice. They just want** quiet."
—Bill Cosby

Never give them anything red to drink!"

Tip submitted by: Amy
Photo submitted by: Karlee

"Dish soap gets **red wine** out of carpet. You would never know there had been a full glass of red wine spilled on our beige carpet. It worked wonders for our relationship with each other and with the offending toddler!"

Tip submitted by: Liz

Remote control + salt = OSM*. "I was six feet away, back turned, washing dishes." *Submitted by: Susan*

*Wondering what "OSM" means? See Epilogue.

"It was when he came into the room and handed me some Rice Krispies that I knew something was wrong."
Submitted by: Elaine

Rocking horse "He got into the Balmex butt paste while I was out shoveling. I call this, 'The White Wonder Horse of Pittsburgh.' " *Submitted by: Gretchen*

Room "We were terrified the twins would kill themselves jumping from one crib to the other, so we put them in toddler beds by the time they were fifteen months old. Of course, they didn't stay in bed. They emptied their dresser drawers and danced in the mess for a couple of hours, eventually falling asleep on the mess by ten p.m. or so."
Submitted by: Alyssa

Room in my own bed
Submitted by: Liberty

"**Rubber** erasers (yep, the plain ol' pink ones) will remove permanent marker from virtually any hard surface, even wood if you move quickly enough. Isopropyl alcohol removes it from computer screens and LCD TV screens without damaging the screens."
Tip submitted by: M.F.S.

Rug "Woke up to find my twin boys rehearsing for the Blue Man Group." Submitted by: S.T.F.

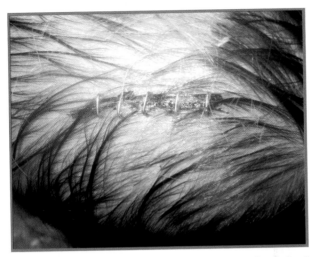

Scalp "Two hours in the ER and five (yes, five) staples later . . .
Well, at least she has an awesome scar story to tell later."
Submitted by: I.C.

On **sanity**:
"Insanity is
hereditary—
you get it from
your children."
—Sam Levenson

blue

Pregnant

pregnant
not pregnant

"My scholarship."
Submitted by: Olive

School supplies "Here fishy, fishy."
Submitted by: Michelle

"Remember those hair **scrunchies**? Do you have any laying around the house collecting dust? Well, instead of getting one of those adult-proof cabinet locks, attach one of these to any lower cabinets that have knobs. Not only can young kids not maneuver these things off the knobs, but it's kinda fun watching them try!"

Tip submitted by: Patty

"Blueberries smuggled into bed stain sheets."
Submitted by: Mia

Sister "My son ruined my daughter's forehead."
Submitted by: Lou

"Get another sitter to watch the husband who is watching the kid."
Tip submitted by: Diana

"Attempting to open the back sliding door."
Submitted by: G.R.

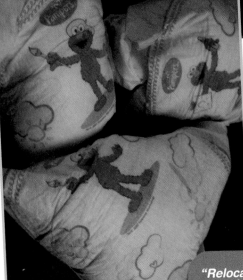

"Having three in diapers has completely ruined the smell of my home."
Submitted by: Amy

"Relocate your chocolate stash every month or so. Also a mild white vinegar and water solution removes chocolate stains."
Submitted by: Mary

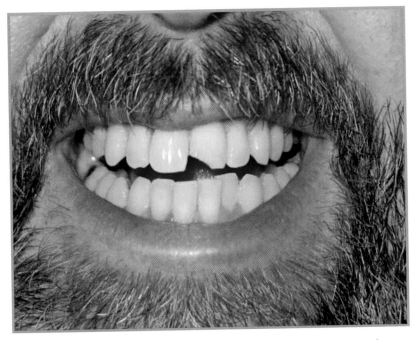

Smile "My daughter decided to head-butt me in the mouth and broke my front tooth. I had to find a new dentist pronto the next day or else look like a goober."
Submitted by: Tedd

"I couldn't help but pull out my camera when I saw him climbing on the table . . . getting the action shot of the entire table doused was a bonus."
Submitted by: Kim

"Few things are more satisfying than seeing your own children have teenagers of their own."
—Doug Larson

"Why there was no pie at our Thanksgiving, circa 2003."
Submitted by: Sharon

"I guess our talks about toy cleanup and toilet training got conflated . . . I submit to you our lovely TOYlet!"
Submitted by: Laura

"My tongue. Now missing a painful chunk after my daughter's giant melon head rocketed up into my jaw."
Submitted by: Paul

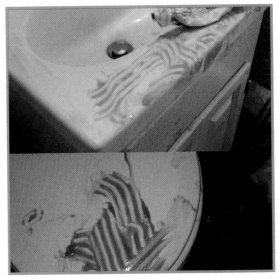

"SMKR: Every single tube of **toothpaste** I buy."
Submitted by: Becky

Truck
Submitted by: Dave

TV "A simple tube of paint in the hands of a three- and a four-year-old . . . people were impressed with the detailed coverage, not me really." *Submitted by: Sally*

"A **two-year-old** is kind of like having a blender, but you don't have a top for it."
—Jerry Seinfeld

Ultrasuede
"Two dozen eggs."
Submitted by:
Cathy

Upholstery "She was supposed to be taking a nap but sang for half an hour instead. Didn't take long to realize why she had been so happy." *Submitted by: Susanna*

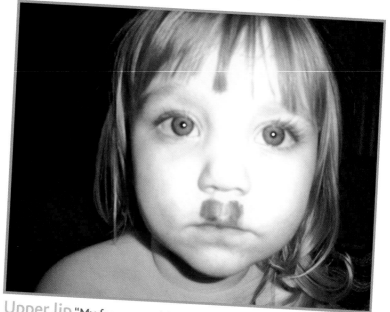

Upper lip "My four-year-old ran in the room telling me that he made his sister into a man . . . he failed to mention that she now looks like a little hatemonger." *Submitted by: Courtney*

Urinary continence
"I can no longer laugh or sneeze without peeing myself."
Submitted by: Greta

"Spray-painted the **van** and each others' backs and hands . . . When asked who did it, they said, 'Not me.'" *Submitted by: Emily*

"My seventeen-month-old twins wanted to watch *Cars* in the **VCR**." *Submitted by: Shelly*

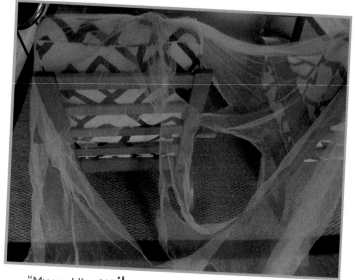

"My wedding **veil**, which I last used ten years ago and no longer need . . . but still. Someone better want to be a ghost for Halloween." *Submitted by: Alexis*

Vertebrae. "Birth ripped the L5/S1 disc apart and resulted in two back surgeries . . . sacral nerve was kinked like a garden hose. Yes, that's as painful as it sounds. Really insane thing? I had another baby two years after this." *Submitted by: Laura*

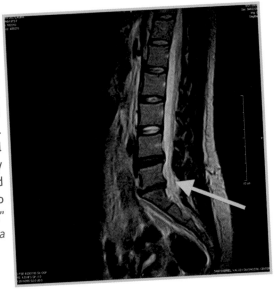

"Vodka removes Sharpie! Scrub with a clean cotton rag or cotton ball soaked in vodka, or splash some vodka onto the surface and let sit for a minute before wiping off. At the very least, it will substantially lighten the mark, and on many materials, it'll remove it completely. I've had the best luck with natural fabrics, plastic, and painted walls. Drink remainder of vodka and repeat."

Submitted by: Maureen

"Here are photos of my twin boys (probably about eighteen months old at the time) ruining my vertical blinds. With great joy, I might add."

Submitted by: Sommer

"My daughter found one of my wife's tubes of lipstick, and decided to write on the wall. When we saw what she was doing we grabbed the camera and 'caught her in the act.' She immediately covered it with her hand and said 'NO NO NO NO NO.' " *Submitted by: Brandon*

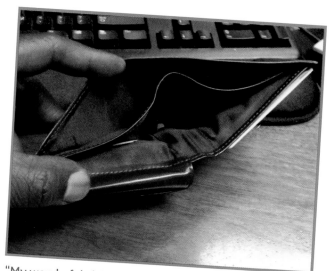

"My wonderful children have thrashed my wallet since the day they were born." *Submitted by: Jim*

Wallpaper

"'Really, you can't do anything—not even something quick like throwing in some laundry or washing a couple of dishes?' Chris asked last night. Yes, really! Here's what happened when I spent 90 seconds in the bathroom today."
Submitted by: Christine

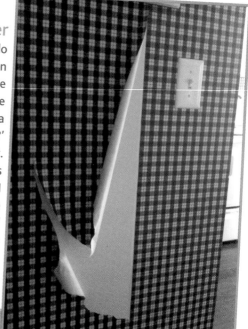

"Cat's water bowl at Grandma's house. My almost-three-year-old's interpretation of a toilet."
Submitted by: Laura

"*Colgate toothpaste (the paste kind) gets ink off of* **white leather.**"

Tip submitted by: Hollie
Photo submitted by: Helene

Wine glass *Submitted by: J.P.B.*

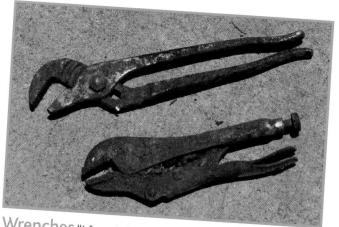

Wrenches "I found these a few months after I asked, 'Did you put my tools away?' This is a payback for all of my dad's tools that I treated the same way." *Submitted by: DeWitte*

X-rated activity "Behold the marital bed!" *Submitted by: PJ*

Yard (back) "Forty-five seconds is all it took for our kids to empty an 8,602.2 gallon pool while I went to check on their mother. She never even had a chance to use the pool. I had spent a week getting it all clean." *Submitted by: Robert*

Yard (front) "I'd like to pretend that this was a tribute to Woodstock instead of a mudpit in my front yard." *Submitted by: Jennifer*

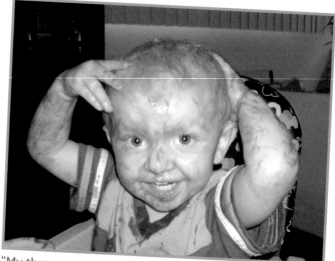

"My then one-year-old thought it would be cool to mix that Twix red and blue **yogurt**." *Submitted by: Jessica*

Younger brother "What your older brother can do to you when he thinks you need a better look." *Submitted by: Monica*

"Our kids have undoubtedly ruined your flight. Sorry."
Submitted by: J.P.B.

ZZZs "Ugh! Just ugh!" *Submitted by: Brynn*

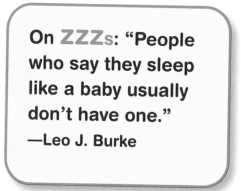

On ZZZs: "People who say they sleep like a baby usually don't have one."
—Leo J. Burke

EPILOGUE

11/14/2009

Photo submitted by: Gina

Wow. Well, that was exhausting! I have to remind myself that each photo came from a different family. But the totality of the kid devastation is certainly impressive.

Something unexpected happens to Shit My Kids Ruined with the passage of time. We look back at these incidents, and where there was once frustration, there's now affection. These become the stories we remember and retell. It turns out that this collection of uncomfortable, unpleasant moments is the substance of life. They are the color, the spice.

A portion of our rug is now framed and hangs in my office. And I look upon our defaced little couch with a fondness I could never have predicted. These have become signifiers of an age and developmental stage gone by. These items, these memories evolve into Shit My Kids Enhanced. With some time and acceptance, I've come to realize that most of what I once deemed *ruined* by my children is, in a sense, *improved*. In the end, it *is* their mark that makes things special.

Silas is OSM

"We sat for days wondering what OSM stood for. Then we realized our five-year-old meant 'Silas is Awesome.' He is." *Submitted by: Lisa*

ACKNOWLEDGMENTS

First and most important, I am grateful to all the families who have submitted photos since the inception of the website. Thank you for sharing your private moments and making *Sh*t My Kids Ruined* work. I mean, my kids can only provide so much material!

To those whose snapshots appear in this book, I offer you special thanks. You endured continual emails from me, some with requests that had you digging deep into old memory cards and computer files and shoeboxes of photographs. Thank you again and I wish you all the very best.

Thank you to my extraordinary team. Richard Pine and Ethan Bassoff of InkWell Management, I am grateful for your help and guidance. I could not have done this without my editor, Marnie Cochran of Ballantine Books. Thank you immensely for this opportunity and for your invaluable direction with this project. I'll never forget our first formal meeting when I arranged nearly 500 pictures of ruined shit around an enormous Random House conference table, and you and I discussed the merits of the cartoon beaver and determined the acceptable amount of poop for this book! The memory will always make me giggle.

I've had the great fortune of support from so many friends and acquaintances, it bowls me over. To you incredible people who first posted about my blog on your Twitter feeds and Facebook pages, I'll never be able to thank you enough for getting the ball rolling. Bloggers Emma Waverman (EmbraceTheChaos.ca) and Nicole Kane Knepper (MomsWhoDrinkAndSwear.com), I thank you for noticing my little site so early on and posting it for your readers. Special thanks goes to Sara Schneider and Elissa Hecker Strauss, two friends who helped the site directly in numerous, imperative ways. And to ALL who encouraged me, and you know who you are, I feel incredibly fortunate to have each one of you in my life—thank you from the depths of my heart.

To my mom and dad, Margot and Ray Haas: I hereby publically acknowledge and apologize for all the shit I sent your way! Thank you for thirty-six years of love and support, and for equipping me with a set of tools with which to do nearly anything. I admire and love and value you immeasurably.

I'm extraordinarily grateful to Brian Haas, my brother, best ally, and now business partner in Sibling Thrivelry, LLC. I love you, and I treasure our friendship and shared humor. There's nobody else on the planet with whom I can imagine collaborating so effectively and trusting so completely all while having fun. You are irreplaceable.

Of all the things for which I can thank my husband, Paul Brophy, it's his seventeen years of encouragement and unwavering confidence in me that has my deepest gratitude. And I think he's cute! I love you, Pablo. I'm proud of you, and our beautiful boys and I are so lucky to have you.

Thank you to our sons for the endless inspiration and support and direction you've given so generously and unknowingly. You make me laugh and beam, and I love you always.

To all the shit-ruining kids across the world: Thank you for providing SMKR with so much fabulous material! You keep the lives of all who love you exciting, exhausting, surprising, and meaningful. Keep it up!

Thank you to the following families for allowing their photos to appear in this book: Alison family, Amber and family, Anderson family, Bagshaw family, Bandelier family, Bateman family, Bauer family, Bayer family, Beasely family, Bell family, Beveridge family, Black family, Bowles family, Brandenberger family, Britvec family, Brosha family, Bundesen family, Cameron family, Cashen family, Child family, Clark family, Cohen family, Cook family, Cooper family, Cramer family, Cronck family, Danas family, Davis family, Derhak family,

Domingue family, Duren family, Eddington family, Edelstein family, Edgerton family, Ernst family, Farrell family, Fletcher family, Force family, Freitas family, Garcia family, Gavel family, Gillmer family, Gros family, Gryphon family, Halpern family, Ham family, Handru-Celestin family, Havenridge family, Hayes family, Helene family, Helmick family, Hershey family, Hix family, Hosford family, Howard family, Hudson family, Hughes family, Jenkins family, Jill family, Jones family, Kat and family, Kelley family, Kelter family, King family, Kinney family, Knell family, Kolasa family, Lappegaard family, Larson family, Lawrence family, LC and family, Lederman-Rowe family, Liberty and family, Lieber family, Lilley family, Little family, Macias family, Mann family, March family, Martinchick family, McCalpin family, McCann family, McClain family, McCormick family, McDonald family, McNaughton family, McPherson family, Moore family, Morgan family, Murray family, Naumovich family, Newman-Shotton family, Nienaber family, Nott family, O'Hearn family, Olive and family, Pave family, Payne family, Peterman family, Porter family, Prestoldt family, Prys family, Puma family, Rachel and family, Radwood family, Rall family, Ramos family, Ray family, Raysor family, Rebecca, Riggs family, Robinson family, Rosier family, Salazar family, Sawyer family, Serpette family, Sheade family, Silverman family, Sladic family, Smith family, Smithson family, Snyder family, Sontag family, Stejskal family, Stewart family, Stone family, Tedd and family, Thimot family, Tireman family, Townsend family, Turnbull family, Tysinger family, Wallace family, Bowie Wankel, Rebecca Weaver, Webb family, Weiss family, White family, Wilson family, Wright family, Yankee family, Zerby family, Zelasko family, and all the other awesome families who submitted photos, tips, and anecdotes. Special thanks to Natasha Duckwall of CaptureByNatasha.com, the only professional photographer whose photo appears in the book.

JULIE HAAS BROPHY is a mother of two, fledgling mosaic artist, and accidental blogger. She earned her BA from Columbia University weeks before turning thirty, and enjoyed more than four years at home with her young sons before creating ShitMyKidsRuined.com. Julie lives with her family in New York.